THE GREAT DEPRESSION AND WORLD WAR II: 1929-1945

by Susan E. Hamen

Content Consultant
Theodore A. Wilson
Professor of History
University of Kansas

CORE LIBRARY

Published by ABDO Publishing Company, PO Box 398166, Minneapolis, MN 55439. Copyright © 2014 by Abdo Consulting Group, Inc. International copyrights reserved in all countries. No part of this book may be reproduced in any form without written permission from the publisher. The Core Library™ is a trademark and logo of ABDO Publishing Company.

Printed in the United States of America,
North Mankato, Minnesota
102013
012014

THIS BOOK CONTAINS AT LEAST 10% RECYCLED MATERIALS.

Editor: Mirella Miller
Series Designer: Becky Daum

Library of Congress Control Number: 2013945674

Cataloging-in-Publication Data
Hamen, Susan E.
 The great depression and World War II: 1929-1945 / Susan E. Hamen.
   p. cm. -- (The story of the United States)
Includes bibliographical references and index.
ISBN 978-1-62403-178-6
1. United States--History--1933-1945--Juvenile literature. 2. United States--History--1919-1933--Juvenile literature. 3. United States--Economic conditions--1918-1945--Juvenile literature. 4. Depressions--1929--United States--Juvenile literature. 5. World War, 1939-1945--United States--Juvenile literature. 6. United States--Social life and customs--To 1945--Juvenile literature. I. Title.
973.917--dc23

2013945674

Photo Credits: AP Images, cover, 1, 4, 9, 12, 17, 20, 23, 32, 34, 37, 45; Library of Congress, 11; John Vachon/Library of Congress, 15; Red Line Editorial, 25, 31; J. Howard Miller, 28; Matty Zimmerman/AP Images, 40

Cover: Many families were forced to stand in food lines during the Great Depression. Homelessness and hunger were common during this era.

CONTENTS

CHAPTER ONE

THE UNITED STATES DURING THE GREAT DEPRESSION

From 1919 to 1929, following World War I (1914–1918), the United States enjoyed a period of increased income, an improved economy, and more social freedoms. World War I was a global war fought mainly in Europe. The United States joined the Allied Powers, which eventually won the war. The period after the war was called the Roaring Twenties.

People crowded onto Wall Street on October 24, 1929, as the stock market crashed.

Clothing became less limiting, and women cut their hair shorter. But would the good times last?

The Stock Market Booms

The stock market allows people to buy shares of stocks in companies. If a business does well, the value of its stock rises and shareholders make money. If a company does poorly, the value of its stock declines and shareholders lose money. During the 1920s, stock market prices climbed. People put large sums of money in the market. They hoped to earn more money as stock prices rose.

The stock market continued to climb until October 1929. Then it experienced losses. People began to sell their stocks. This brought the prices of stocks down further. On October 24, 1929, the stock market crashed. Many people panicked and sold their stocks. This caused people to lose money. By October 29, investors had sold more than 16 million shares of stocks. People lost huge sums of money.

This crash marked the beginning of the Great Depression.

The Great Depression

The stock market crash threw the United States into an economic mess. Millions of people lost their life savings. Nearly 15 million Americans were without jobs by 1933. Those who had jobs were making far less money than before. Many Americans found it hard to buy the basic necessities, such as food. Families sold cars, furniture, and other objects to make money. Hunger and homelessness became common across

The Automobile Industry

Before 1919 there were fewer than 5 million cars in the United States. By 1929 that number had grown to approximately 23 million. This meant more roadways were needed. It also created a need for gas stations, restaurants, and tire stores. Automobiles helped create more jobs for Americans. But like other industries, the automobile industry collapsed during the Great Depression.

the country. Millions of factory workers were told they no longer had jobs.

Farmers also suffered when the Great Depression began. Crop prices were already low. These prices dropped even further since people could not afford food. This meant farmers did not make money. They were unable to pay their bills. Many farmers had taken out loans with banks. Banks took farms away from families who could not repay their loans. Thousands of banks eventually went out of business.

The Dust Bowl

Things continued to get worse. In 1931 a horrible drought hit Oklahoma, Texas, Kansas, New Mexico, and Colorado. Farmers in these states had planted the same crops year after year. This damaged the soil.

When the drought came, the top layer of nutrient-rich soil was blown away. Dust storms moved across the states in 1932. Black dirt was blown all around and covered everything. These states became known as the Dust Bowl. This land could no longer be

A dust cloud moves toward a farm in Oklahoma. The dust made it impossible for farmers to plant or grow crops.

EXPLORE ONLINE

The focus in Chapter One was on the Dust Bowl. The Web site below discusses the Dust Bowl. As you know, every source is different. How is the information on the Web site different from the information in this chapter? What information is the same? How do the two sources present information differently? What can you learn from this Web site?

Surviving the Dust Bowl

www.mycorelibrary.com/great-depression-and-world-war-ii

used to grow crops. Many farm families moved west to find work.

A New President

The nation was in despair, and no end seemed to be in sight. In 1931 President Herbert Hoover assured Americans the worst was behind them. But poverty continued to rise. Some families lived in shacks they built. Many Americans still did not have jobs. The nation was in the worst economic situation it had ever experienced.

President Franklin D. Roosevelt, *right*, hoped to help the country out of its bad economic situation. Former president Hoover, *left*, had been unable to help the country recover during his presidency.

Americans were ready for a change. Franklin D. Roosevelt won the 1932 presidential election. He promised to help the country. Americans hoped he would be able to bring the change they needed.

CHAPTER TWO

THE NEW DEAL

President Roosevelt knew he could not waste time taking action. He was determined to turn the country around. Roosevelt created the New Deal. The New Deal was a series of government programs put into place from 1933 to 1936. These programs were designed to provide relief to the country.

Immediately after becoming president, Roosevelt proclaimed a national bank holiday.

President Roosevelt passed the Emergency Banking Act in 1933 as the first part of the New Deal.

On March 6, 1933, all banks closed their doors. The US Congress met during this time. It passed a bill called the Emergency Banking Act. This marked the first step in Roosevelt's New Deal. This bill, and several others, helped stabilize the banks. It also gave the US Treasury the power to print more money.

Federal Emergency Relief Act

The next step in Roosevelt's New Deal was to help people get jobs. Jobs would provide workers with paychecks they could use for food, shelter, and clothing.

In April 1933 the Civilian Conservation Corps (CCC) was formed to put young men to work

Works Progress Administration

On May 6, 1935, the Federal Emergency Relief Act (FERA) became the Works Progress Administration (WPA). The WPA received money to provide Americans with wages. The WPA employed more than 8.5 million workers over eight years. Along with the Public Works Administration, the WPA constructed thousands of public buildings, bridges, and playgrounds.

The CCC gave nearly 3 million men between the ages of 18 and 25 jobs.

on outdoor projects. The CCC improved national parks by planting nearly 3 billion trees. CCC workers also cleared hiking paths. The young men lived in barracks and received $30 per month.

The Federal Emergency Relief Act (FERA) was passed on May 12, 1933. FERA provided food, clothing, and shelter for people. This act also sponsored work programs. Millions of Americans built roads, schools, parks, and sewers under FERA.

Farmers Receive Assistance

President Roosevelt and his administration knew they needed to address the farm crisis. Congress passed the Agricultural Adjustment Act on May 13, 1933. This act helped reduce extra crops and drive prices up. Farmers received money from the government to not plant fields and to destroy existing crops. Farmers were finally earning enough money to survive.

Electricity in the Rural South

Congress created the Tennessee Valley Authority (TVA) in 1933. It was created to help with environmental, economic, and technological issues. The TVA also helped build a hydroelectric power plant. The TVA contributed to the economic development in the South.

Help for Students

The New Deal also included programs designed to help students. The Great Depression forced many young people to drop out of high school and college to earn money for their families. The National Youth Administration

The TVA constructed dams to prevent the flooding of the Tennessee River.

(NYA) was formed in 1935. It offered grants to high school and college students. These young people worked part-time jobs in exchange for money for school. They often worked in libraries or as janitors. The NYA allowed millions of students to remain in school while earning wages.

The Beginning of Social Security

Hardly anyone was able to save for retirement during the Great Depression. People who were too old to work lived with relatives.

The Social Security Act of 1935 was meant to fix this problem. It provided Americans past the age of 65 with an income after they stopped working. Employed Americans paid into the program through taxes. This money then went to those who needed social security benefits. This was the beginning of the social welfare system in the United States.

Not everyone agreed with the programs President Roosevelt helped establish. Some programs worked better than others. But Roosevelt believed it was important to try everything to help the country.

President Roosevelt gave regular speeches, known as fireside chats. He delivered them by radio from the White House. This excerpt from May 7, 1933, explains the progress the United States had made since the stock market crash:

> *Today we have reason to believe that things are a little better than they were two months ago. Industry has picked up, railroads are carrying more freight, farm prices are better. . . . We are working toward a definite goal, which is to prevent the return of conditions, which came very close to destroying what we call modern civilization. The actual accomplishment of our purpose cannot be attained in a day. . . . We are encouraged to believe that a wise and sensible beginning has been made. In the present spirit of mutual confidence and mutual encouragement we go forward.*
>
> Source: "Outlining the New Deal Program." May 7, 1933. Fireside Chats of Franklin D. Roosevelt. *Mid-Hudson Regional Information Center, n.d. Web. Accessed September 13, 2013.*

What's the Big Idea?

Take a close look at President Roosevelt's words. What is his main idea? What evidence does he use to support his point? Come up with a few sentences showing how President Roosevelt uses two or three pieces of evidence to support his main point.

CHAPTER THREE

THE UNITED STATES ENTERS WORLD WAR II

The United States was not the only country experiencing difficult times. The effects of the Great Depression were felt around the world. Europe was still struggling with the destruction from World War I. More than 16 million Europeans had lost their lives. Twenty-one million suffered injuries. Many countries were destroyed.

On September 1, 1939, Adolf Hitler ordered the German army to invade Poland. This marked the beginning of World War II.

The Rise of Hitler and the Nazi Party

Adolf Hitler promised the struggling people of Germany he could help re-establish jobs. Hitler was the leader of the National Socialist German Workers' Party, also known as the Nazi Party. On January 30, 1933, Hitler became chancellor of Germany. He eventually combined the positions of chancellor and president. This made Hitler the sole leader of Germany. He was called the *Führer*, or leader.

Hitler wanted to rebuild Germany's military. To increase Germany's power, Hitler wanted to attack other European countries. Hitler also wanted to rid Germany of any minorities. He viewed other races and cultures as inferior. He believed these groups were to blame for Germany's problems. By the late 1930s, the country was on the verge of another deadly war.

World War II Begins

On September 1, 1939, Hitler's troops attacked Poland. This marked the beginning of World War II

Hitler, center, spent large amounts of money to rebuild Germany's military.

(1939–1945). Two days later, France and Great Britain responded by declaring war against Germany. They formed the beginning of the Allied Powers. France and Great Britain knew Hitler could eventually attack their own countries. He had to be stopped.

War continued to rage through Europe as Hitler's troops attacked Norway and France. The Battle of Britain was fought in the air during the summer and fall of 1940. German planes dropped bombs over British soil. But Great Britain's Royal Air Force kept Germany from invading Great Britain. In 1940 Hitler entered into an alliance with Italy and Japan, forming

Air Raids and Evacuation

Great Britain endured massive bombings during the Battle of Britain. Sirens screamed out warnings for British civilians to take cover as German planes dropped bombs. Parents evacuated their children from the cities. They sent them on trains to live with strangers in rural areas. Siblings were often split up.

the Axis Powers. He also sent Jewish people and other minorities to concentration camps. There they were forced to work. Millions were put to death.

In June 1941, Germany attacked the Soviet Union. Nearly all of Europe was at war. The death toll rose daily. Many others lost their homes and land. Families were split apart, and destruction lay everywhere.

The United States' Help

The United States was not ready to enter into a second world war. But after the fall of France in June 1940, the US War Department sent guns and planes to the British. Later they sent 50 destroyer ships.

Europe During World War II

This map shows how Europe was divided during World War II. It shows which countries were a part of the Axis Powers. It also shows which countries fought with the Allies. Countries that came under Axis Powers control are also on the map. Look at the map and think about the countries that Hitler attacked. Where are they located in comparison to Germany? Why is this important?

Although the United States was not yet fighting in World War II, it was helping the effort to fight Nazi Germany.

Pearl Harbor

Early in the morning on December 7, 1941, Japanese fighter and bomber planes attacked the

US Hawaiian naval base. The following day, the United States responded by declaring war on Japan. Germany, Japan's ally, then declared war on the United States. The United States was once again at war. It became an official member of the Allied Powers against the Axis Powers.

A War on Two Fronts

In November 1942, US soldiers were sent overseas. Under General Dwight D. Eisenhower, the US Army, along with British and French troops, battled the Germans. The US Navy was also fighting Japan in the Pacific Ocean. The ships that survived the Pearl Harbor bombings

Pearl Harbor Caught Off Guard

When the Japanese attacked Pearl Harbor, Americans stationed at the bases were caught off guard. Many were not even out of bed yet. At Kaneohe Bay's Naval Air Station, a cook ran through the barracks, banging a spoon against a cake pan to wake the pilots. Pilots ran to their planes still dressed in their pajamas. Sailors rushed to their ships.

FURTHER EVIDENCE

There is a lot of information in Chapter Three about the countries involved in World War II. What is the main point of the chapter? What evidence is given to support that point? Visit the Web site below to learn more about the countries and areas of the world that were affected by World War II. Choose a quote from the Web site that relates to this chapter. Does the quote support the author's point about World War II? Write a few sentences explaining how the quote you found relates to this chapter.

World War II
www.mycorelibrary.com/great-depression-and-world-war-ii

moved west to attack Japanese military bases in the central Pacific Ocean.

President Roosevelt worked together with Great Britain's Prime Minister, Winston Churchill, and Russia's leader, Joseph Stalin. They combined forces against Germany, Italy, and Japan. It would be a long, bloody struggle before either side could claim victory.

We Can Do It!

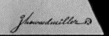

POST FEB. 15 TO FEB. 28

CHAPTER FOUR

ON THE HOME FRONT

The United States needed to expand and arm its military for war. Factories worked quickly to create weapons, ammunition, tanks, and many other items for the war effort.

In 1940 a peacetime draft was introduced. It called young men to fight for the US military. This left a shortage of workers for factories and other industries. The government began to encourage

Advertisements featuring Rosie the Riveter encouraged women to help out with the war effort.

women to help the war effort by entering the work force.

Throughout World War II, the number of women working outside the home rose from 12 to 18 million. Many took positions typing and filing. Others worked in factories putting together airplanes and tanks. They also helped produce weapons and bullets.

Making Do

The US military needed more than guns, tanks, and airplanes. They needed nylon and silk for parachutes and military uniforms. Metal, rubber, and leather were also in short supply due to military priorities. Americans at home had trouble getting everything from shoes to chocolate.

The US government created a ration system to deal with the shortage of goods. Rationing limited how much of an item people could purchase. Sugar, cheese, and meat were rationed. To make up for the shortage of ingredients, women became creative with recipes. People planted victory gardens.

Food Item	Can Size	Ration Points
Soup	10.5 oz.	6 points
Fruit Cocktail	1 lb. 1 oz.	11 points
Corn	1 lb. 4 oz.	14 points
Peas	1 lb. 4 oz.	16 points
Tomatoes	1 lb. 3 oz.	16 points
Peaches	1 lb. 14 oz.	21 points
Pears	1 lb. 14 oz.	21 points
Pineapple Juice	2 lb. 14 oz.	32 points
Tomato Juice	2 lb. 14 oz.	32 points

Ration Points

This chart gives an example of ration points. Each month every person in a household was given a certain number of canned goods points. If you had 48 points to use on canned goods, how would you spend your points for the month? How long do you think the canned foods you chose would last? How does this chart help you better understand limited resources and food during World War II?

These gardens helped increase the amount of food available. Even fashions changed during the war. The lack of available cloth led to shorter skirts and simpler men's suits.

During World War II, approximately 120,000 Japanese Americans were moved to war relocation camps, such as this one in California.

National Pride

Men, women, and children contributed to the war effort. Neighborhoods collected old metal parts to recycle for war needs. Children collected cans, bottle caps, and other scraps of metal. People traveled very little since gasoline was hard to get. Americans pulled together showing unity and national pride. They worked hard to save resources and support the war.

The Fate of Japanese Americans

While most Americans pulled together, they held onto a fear about Japanese Americans. After the bombing by Japan at Pearl Harbor, Americans were uneasy.

A majority of Japanese Americans living on the West Coast were born in the United States. But Americans still worried they might have strong loyalties to Japan.

An order issued by President Roosevelt in 1942 forced Japanese Americans to leave their homes. They were moved to war relocation camps. Most of these Japanese Americans lost their jobs, homes, and possessions.

Other minorities also felt left out of the feelings of pride that grew across the country. While African-American men were drafted in the military, they had less important roles. They were unable to move up through the ranks. Segregation continued in the military and at home during the war.

War Relocation Camps

Ten war relocation camps were built in Arizona, Arkansas, California, Colorado, Idaho, Utah, and Wyoming. The conditions of these camps were horrific. The camps were located in isolated areas.

CHAPTER FIVE

VICTORY!

The United States entered the war in December 1941. For nearly four years, US soldiers fought alongside other Allied Powers to keep German troops from advancing. Americans back home provided the soldiers with weapons and support.

US troops wade ashore in Normandy, France, on June 6, 1944, to attack German troops.

D-Day

In early 1943, British and US pilots began bombing German cities. They destroyed factories that produced war materials for Germany.

On the morning of June 6, 1944, General Eisenhower ordered a joint attack on German-held France. More than 150,000 US, British, and Canadian troops and naval ships were brought together on the shores of Normandy, France. Soldiers hurried to make it to the beach through the choppy waters. German machine guns and land mines met them. Hundreds of men died instantly as the beach exploded.

This battle was known as D-Day. The Allies lost 5,000 men, but Germany suffered greater losses. The D-Day victory allowed the Allies to move into France and push the Germans out. This meant France was finally free from Nazi Party occupation.

V-E Day

In March 1945, US, British, and French troops made their way to the German border. Realizing his plan

In the weeks that followed D-Day, more than 1 million Allied Powers soldiers poured into Europe through Normandy.

to conquer Europe had failed, Adolf Hitler took his own life on April 30, 1945. The Nazi Party's reign was over. The Allies won the war in Europe. On

The Death of President Roosevelt

Many of President Roosevelt's New Deal programs helped the United States during the Great Depression. Roosevelt also led the country through the struggles of World War II. On April 12, 1945, President Roosevelt died just weeks before World War II ended in Europe. The nation mourned the passing of a great leader.

May 7, 1945, Germany surrendered to Allied Powers. The following day was declared VE Day, which meant Victory in Europe Day.

Japan is Defeated

Although the battle in Europe came to an end, fighting against Japan continued. When Japan refused to surrender, the United States took drastic measures. On August 6, 1945, a US airplane dropped an atomic bomb on Hiroshima, Japan. The blast killed 70,000 people instantly. The radiation given off by the bomb killed another 30,000.

Three days later, the United States dropped a second atomic bomb on Nagasaki, Japan. Another 35,000 to 40,000 Japanese were killed. On September 2, 1945, Japan signed surrender documents. World War II was finally over.

After the War

Following the war, soldiers came back to their prewar jobs. The majority of women left the workforce and returned to their homes. Some women remained employed.

In the 16 years following the stock market crash of 1929, the United States struggled economically but eventually emerged from the Great Depression.

Concentration Camps

The true horror of Nazi Germany's concentration camps was finally realized at the end of the war. Allied Powers troops freed more than 80,000 prisoners from different camps. Thousands of prisoners were so weak, they died shortly after the war. Soldiers also found the bodies of hundreds of thousands of people at the camps.

Soldiers returned home as war heroes to parades and happy family and friends.

Hunger and homelessness was a thing of the past. Factories and industry were alive and producing goods. The achievements of President Roosevelt's New Deal and the war effort of World War II made the United States a prosperous nation once again.

The defeat of Germany was a victory celebrated around the world. This excerpt from the *New York Times* announced Germany's surrender:

> *Germany surrendered unconditionally to the Western Allies and the Soviet Union at 2:41 A.M. French time today.*
>
> *The surrender . . . brought the war in Europe to a formal end after five years, eight months and six days of bloodshed and destruction.*
>
> *Germans Say They Understand Terms*
>
> *They were asked sternly if they understand the surrender terms imposed upon Germany and if they would be carried out by Germany.*
>
> *They answered Yes.*
>
> Source: Edward Kennedy. "The War in Europe is Ended! Surrender Is Unconditional." New York Times, May 8, 1945. Web. Accessed September 13, 2013.

Consider Your Audience

Review this excerpt closely. How would you change it for a different audience, such as your parents or younger friends? Write a blog post explaining this same information to the new audience. How does your approach differ from the original text and why?

IMPORTANT DATES

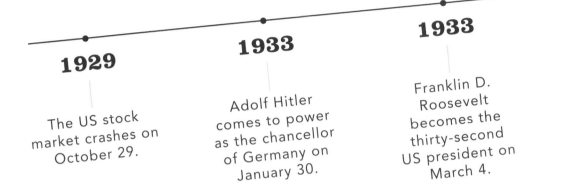

1929

The US stock market crashes on October 29.

1933

Adolf Hitler comes to power as the chancellor of Germany on January 30.

1933

Franklin D. Roosevelt becomes the thirty-second US president on March 4.

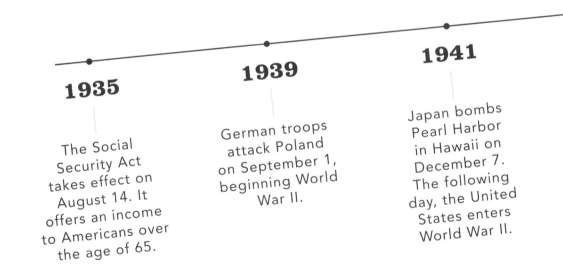

1935

The Social Security Act takes effect on August 14. It offers an income to Americans over the age of 65.

1939

German troops attack Poland on September 1, beginning World War II.

1941

Japan bombs Pearl Harbor in Hawaii on December 7. The following day, the United States enters World War II.

1933

The Civilian Conservation Corps (CCC) is formed on April 5 to put young men to work on outdoor projects.

1933

The Federal Emergency Relief Act (FERA) is passed on May 12.

1933

On May 13, the Agricultural Adjustment Act is passed to help farmers.

1944

On June 6, Allied Powers troops storm the beaches of Normandy, France, in a battle known as D-Day.

1945

Germany surrenders to the Allies on May 7.

1945

Japan surrenders to the United States on September 2, ending World War II.

Why Do I Care?

This book discusses the Great Depression and World War II, which happened in the last century. Even though you did not experience the Great Depression or World War II, how does this history affect your life? Write down two or three ways this era connects to your life.

You Are There

Chapter Three discusses Nazi Party troops entering towns. This was an especially scary time for many Europeans. Imagine you are a young European girl or boy. The Nazi Party troops have just attacked a neighboring town. How might your family react to the news? Do you stay in your home or flee? How might your decision change if your family is Jewish?

Say What?

This era of US history presents a lot of new vocabulary. Find five words in this book that you've never heard before. Use a dictionary to learn what they mean. Then write the meanings in your own words. Use each word in a new sentence.

Surprise Me

Learning about life during World War II can be interesting and surprising. Think about what you learned from this book. Can you name two or three facts in this book that surprised you? Write a short paragraph about each fact. Describe what you found surprising about the fact and why.

GLOSSARY

barracks
buildings used to lodge soldiers

chancellor
the chief minister of state in some European countries

concentration camp
a camp with horrible conditions where prisoners of war are sent

draft
a system of selecting individuals for required military service

Führer
a German word that means "leader"

grant
a gift of money that does not need to be repaid

land mine
a mine placed just under the surface of the ground, which explodes when driven over or stepped on

radiation
dangerous energy given off by a radioactive blast that can severely burn, injure, and kill

ration
a limit placed on certain food items or goods

stock
a share of a publicly held company or the total shares issued by a company

LEARN MORE

Books

Adams, Simon. *World War II*. New York: Dorling Kindersley Limited, 2010.

Gitlin, Martin. *The 1929 Stock Market Crash*. Minneapolis: ABDO, 2008.

Hamen, Susan E. *The New Deal*. Minneapolis: ABDO, 2011.

Web Links

To learn more about the Great Depression and WWII, visit ABDO Publishing Company online at **www.abdopublishing.com**. Web sites about this era are featured on our Book Links page. These links are routinely monitored and updated to provide the most current information available.

Visit **www.mycorelibrary.com** for free additional tools for teachers and students.

INDEX

ABOUT THE AUTHOR

Susan E. Hamen is a full-time editor and freelance writer. She has written books on various topics, including the Wright brothers, the Industrial Revolution, and Germany. Hamen lives in Minnesota with her husband and two children.